Ralph Vaughan Wi...

THE EARLY WORKS

String Quartet in C minor

(1 8 9 8)

FABER *ff* MUSIC

Set of parts ISBN 0-571-52176-2
Score ISBN 0-571-52085-5

Duration: *c*.25 minutes

The String Quartet in C minor is recorded by The Nash Ensemble
on the 2-CD album from Hyperion
'Ralph Vaughan Williams: The Early Chamber Music' CDA67381/2

To buy Faber Music publications or to find out about the full range of titles available
please contact your local music retailer or Faber Music sales enquiries:

Faber Music Ltd, Burnt Mill, Elizabeth Way, Harlow CM20 2HX
Tel: +44 (0)1279 82 89 82   Fax: +44 (0)1279 82 89 83
sales@fabermusic.com   fabermusic.com

INTRODUCTORY NOTE

This work was composed in 1897–8 when Vaughan Williams was 25. He had married Adeline Fisher in October 1897 and during part of their honeymoon in Germany he had some composition lessons from Max Bruch. At home he was the organist of St Barnabas, Lambeth, which he found uncongenial work. His compositions up to this date had mainly been songs or pieces for mixed chorus. Apart from two prentice piano trios, he had written no chamber music. The String Quartet, perhaps inspired by the example of a similar work by his friend Nicholas Gatty, was therefore his first major composition of any kind, so its accomplishment is all the more remarkable. It was performed for the first time at the Oxford and Cambridge Musical Club on 30 January 1904 and not again, so far as is known, until a student quartet at the Royal College of Music, London, performed it on 15 March 2002.

The autograph manuscript was among the large collection presented to the British Library by Ursula Vaughan Williams after her husband's death in 1958. The unpublished early works carried an embargo forbidding performance, in accordance with the composer's wishes. But after 40 years, in consultation with her advisers and in view of the interest being expressed in the music Vaughan Williams wrote before about 1908, she agreed to the publication and performance of certain selected works. This String Quartet has been prepared for publication by Bernard Benoliel, project controller and editorial consultant, in collaboration with the editorial staff of Faber Music.

Michael Kennedy

String Quartet in C minor

(1898)

Ralph Vaughan Williams
(1872-1958)

VIOLIN I

I Allegro

II

Ralph Vaughan Williams

THE EARLY WORKS

String Quartet
in C minor

(1898)

First published in 2002 by Faber Music Ltd
3 Queen Square London WC1N 3AU
Music processed by Christopher Hinkins
Cover design by S & M Tucker
Printed in England by Caligraving Ltd

Set of parts ISBN 0-571-52176-2

Duration: *c.*25 minutes

FABER *ff* MUSIC

String Quartet in C minor

(1898)

Ralph Vaughan Williams
(1872-1958)

VIOLIN II

I Allegro

Allegro ♩. = 76

[musical notation]

II

III Intermezzo

IV Variazione con finale fugato

VARIATION VI (minore)

Allegro

FINALE FUGATO

Allegro moderato

Ralph Vaughan Williams

THE EARLY WORKS

String Quartet
in C minor

(1898)

Duration: *c*.25 minutes

String Quartet in C minor

(1898)

Ralph Vaughan Williams
(1872-1958)

VIOLA

I Allegro

VIOLA

III Intermezzo

IV Variazione con finale fugato

Ralph Vaughan Williams

THE EARLY WORKS

String Quartet
in C minor

(1898)

Set of parts ISBN 0-571-52176-2

Duration: *c*.25 minutes

FABER ff MUSIC

String Quartet in C minor

(1898)

CELLO

Ralph Vaughan Williams
(1872-1958)

I Allegro

CELLO

II

III Intermezzo

TRIO

IV Variazione con finale fugato

THEME
Allegro moderato ♩ = 132

[*attacca*]

VARIATION I

VARIATION II
Adagio
f largamente

cresc.

Left blank to facilitate page turns

VARIATION V (maggiore)
Con moto ma non troppo

VARIATION VI (minore)
Allegro

FINALE FUGATO

III Intermezzo

IV Variazione con finale fugato

THEME
Allegro moderato ♩ = 132

[*attacca*]

VARIATION I

FINALE FUGATO
Allegro moderato